SMART, STRONG, & BRAVE

A COLORING BOOK FOR GIRLS

www.castlepointbooks.com

The Castle Point Books trademark is owned by Castle Point Publishing, LLC.
Castle Point books are published and distributed by St. Martin's Press.

Illustration by Kimma Parish.

ISBN 978-1-250-27227-0 (trade paperback)

Our books may be purchased in bulk for promotional, educational, or business
use. Please contact your local bookseller or the Macmillan Corporate and
Premium Sales Department at 1-800-221-7945, extension 5442,
or by email at MacmillanSpecialMarkets@macmillan.com.

First Edition: 2020

10 9 8 7 6 5 4 3 2 1

SMART, STRONG, & BRAVE

A COLORING BOOK FOR GIRLS

ILLUSTRATIONS BY KIMMA PARISH

CASTLE POINT BOOKS

NEW YORK

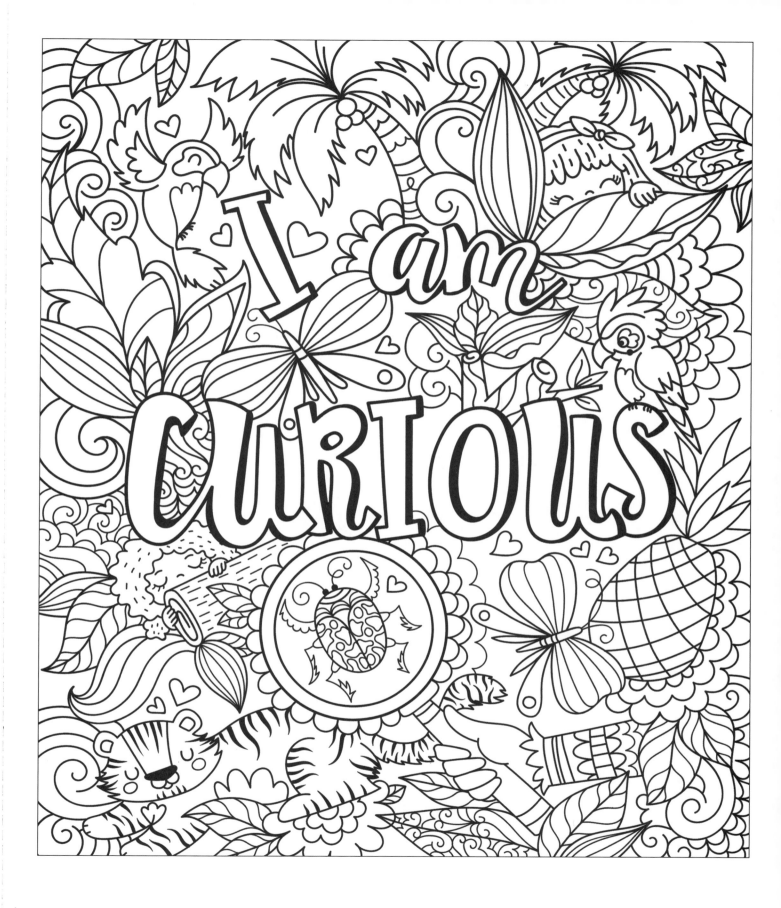

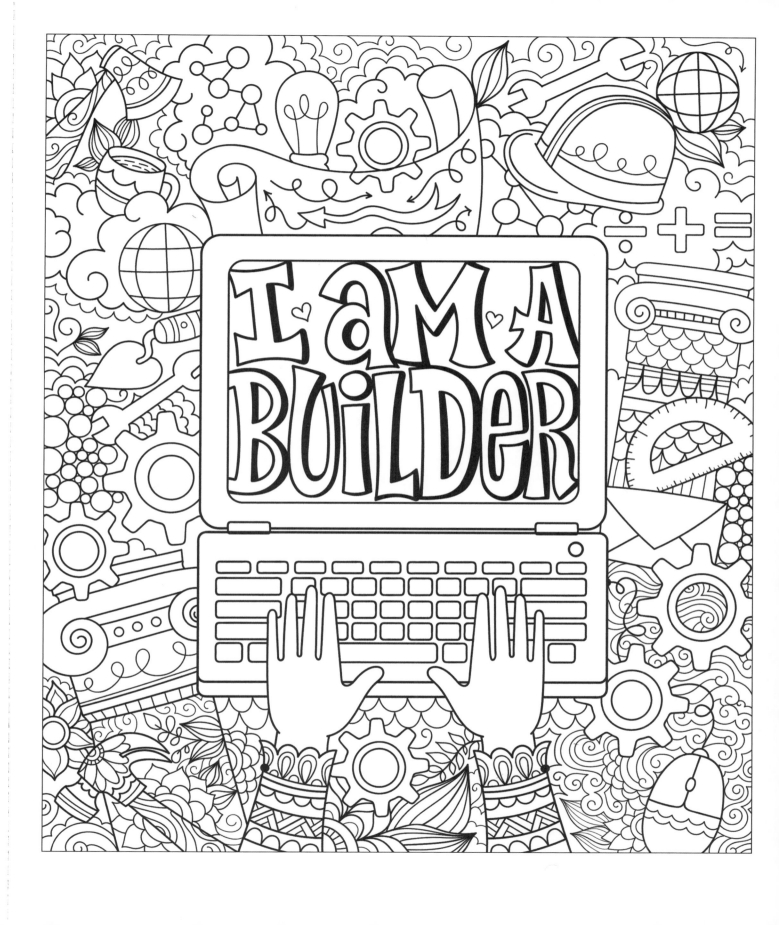

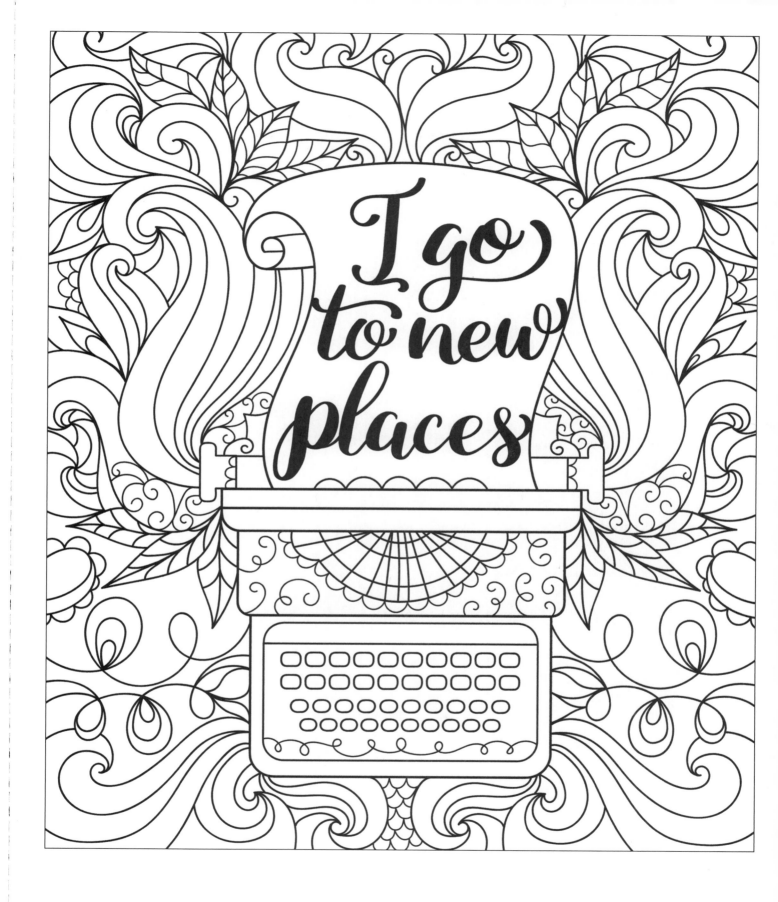

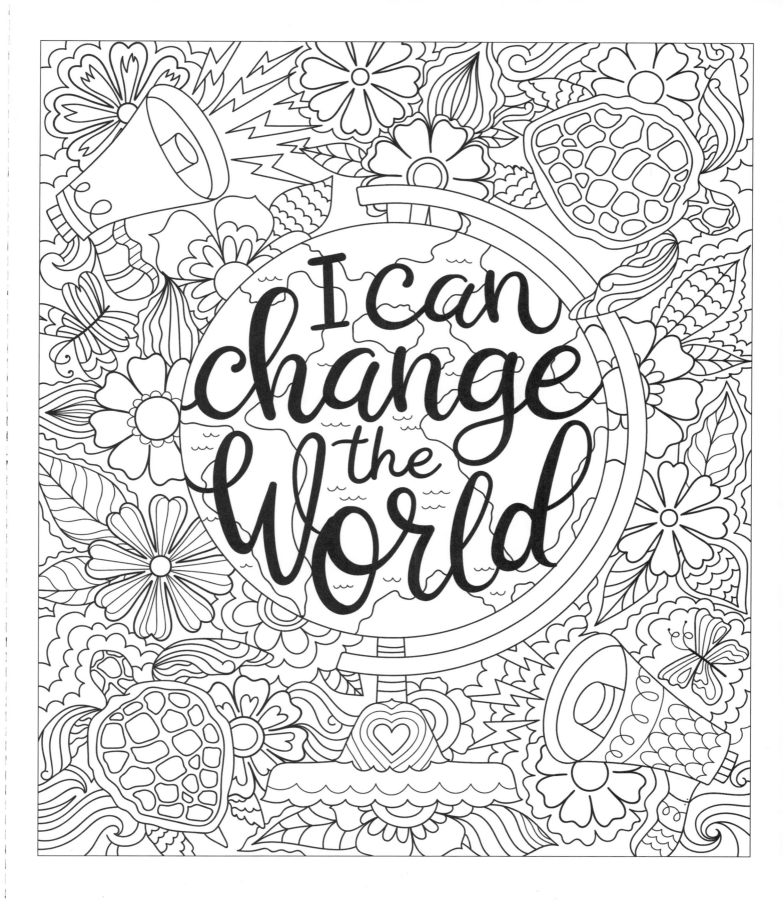

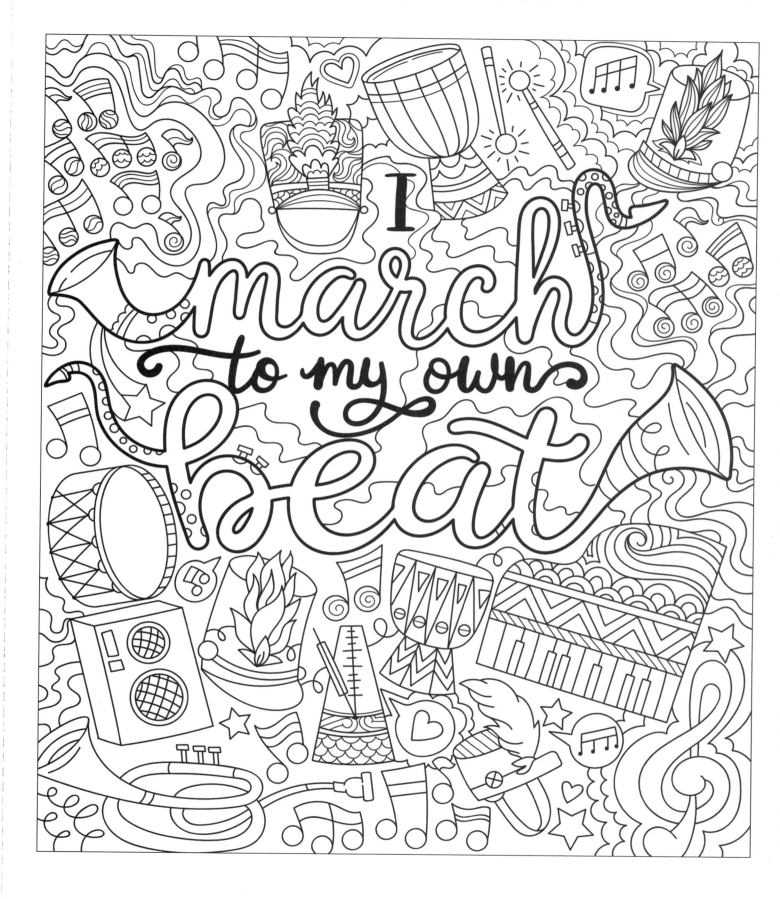

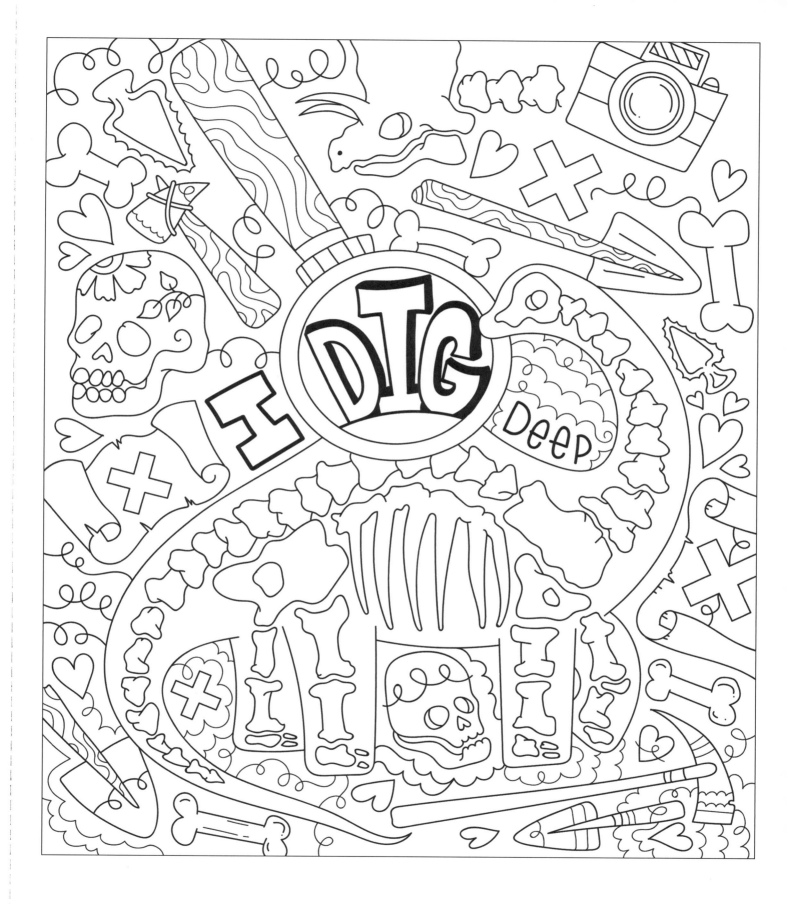

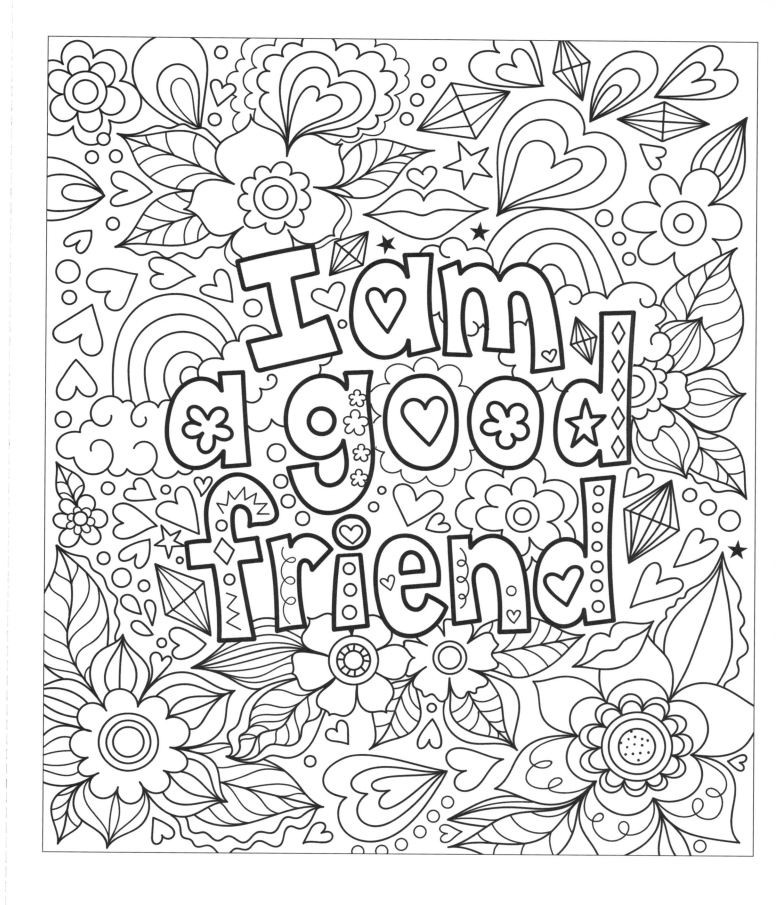

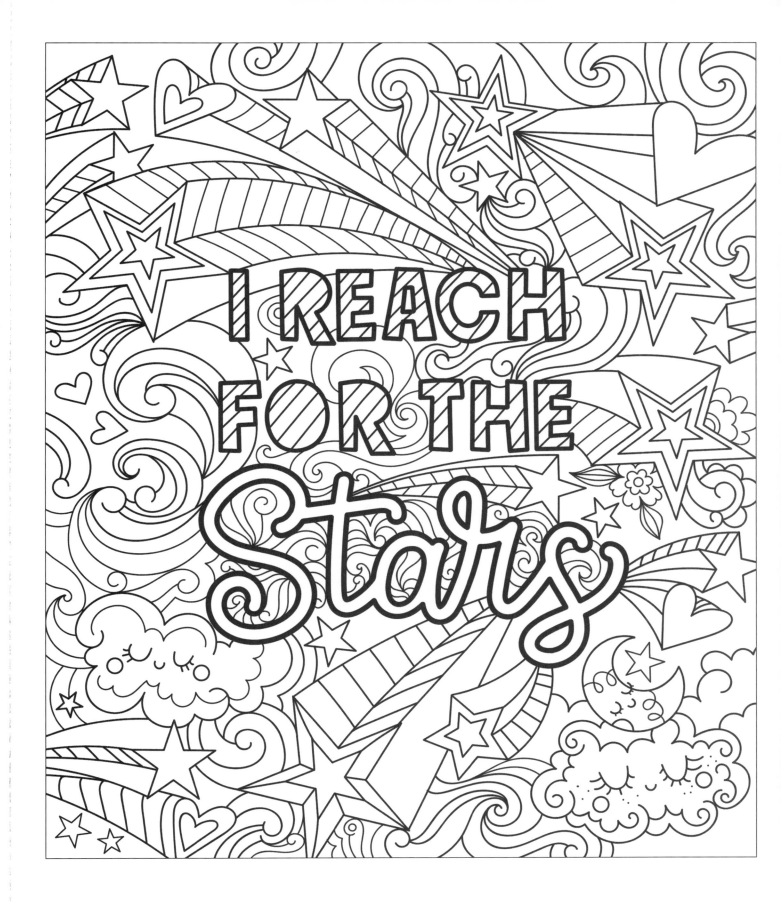